A
GOOD BOOK

COOK BOOK

WENDY BARRIE

SCO⧫ISH
BIBLE SOCIETY
The Word for the world

Contents

Recipes for a Buffet

Recipes for Dining

The Selkirk Grace

Some hae meat and canna eat,
And some wad eat that want it;
But we hae meat, and we can eat,
And sae the Lord be thankit.

Published by The Scottish Bible Society
7 Hampton Terrace, Edinburgh EH12 5XU
© Scottish Bible Society 2007
No part of this publication may be reproduced or transmitted in any form or by any means, electronic or mechanical, including photocopying, recording or any information storage or retrieval system, without permission in writing from the publisher.
Recipes by Wendy Barrie (wendy@scottishfoodguide.com)
Photographs by Tony Gorzkowski (tony@whitehousestudios.co.uk)
Edited by John Lloyd
Cover and text design by Eric Drewery (eric.drewery@virgin.net)
All Scripture texts are taken from the New Revised Standard Version
Printed in Great Britain by Meigle Colour Printers Ltd

FOREWORD BY THE REVD. JULIE WILSON

Are you of the 'little and often' or 'three square meals a day and nothing in between' brigade? I love good food. But I would rather preach a sermon to hundreds of people than cook up dinner for six. I am challenged, therefore, by Jesus' use of meals as a forum for teaching.

I've decided that the best way forward for me is to make my kitchen available for those who can cook. I'm then happy to lay the table and sit down with friends to enjoy what is on offer!

Flick through the pages of Luke's Gospel and you will find Jesus eating! Eating with his disciples, eating with outsiders, eating with religious leaders. Look at the parables Jesus told – there are banquets and wedding feasts, scraps from the table, food for pigs and loaves from neighbours. Think of the times Jesus sat at a table as a guest – in the homes of Simon, Matthew, Martha and Mary, Cleopas. Then remember the time he was most definitely the host, sharing a final meal with his friends, before becoming the meal itself in the bread and wine.

As Jesus eats, he brings transformation, welcome to the outcast and challenge to the pompous. As he sits at the table, Jesus teaches – bringing spiritual nourishment. When Jesus spoke of his Kingdom, he used language we can all understand … it's like a banquet!

In our culture of fast food, ready meals and easy options, lingering over a homemade meal is seen as a luxury, the reserve of special occasions. Little wonder then that we are undernourished in our relationships and frequently suffer indigestion from our own opinions.

Pause with Jesus as he dines.

May this little book be the 'starter' for a new approach to our dining – where Kingdom values are reflected and where we savour a foretaste of the meal that is to come!

INTRODUCTION BY WENDY BARRIE

In the beginning there was food. Without it there would have been no Good Book and no inspiration for A Good Book Cook Book. Fortunately God's Grand Design provided all creatures with the staff of life, to survive and procreate. But for most species food is more than an essential fuel. It aids family and community bonding and in human societies there are even special days when certain foods complement the occasion, are themselves the object of celebration or even of ritual abstinence.

Recently I was among a large group of producers, farmers, fishermen and cooks, invited to share experiences at the Slow Food movement's Terra Madre, a world meeting of food communities, in Italy. Each day, time was allotted to a regional 'talk local' session. On the day of the Middle Eastern communities there was a noticeable unease in the air as delegates, normally the worst of enemies, assembled. A giant plaited loaf of bread had been prepared and every person broke off a piece and dipped it in salt in an ancient symbolism of peace. There followed an inspiring meeting, closing with much friendship, shaking of hands and embracing. For me this moving experience bore testament to the de-stressing potential of food in times of trouble.

A Good Book Cook Book is not intended to put the world to rights but will be a journey back to Biblical times in search of food traditions and the religious and social mores which influenced them. It will bring together recipes, some suited to open fires and barbecues, most giving practical instructions for today's kitchens and using ingredients akin to Biblical time and place and reflecting the manner in which the produce would have been used.

Here I offer a taster of recipes that can be prepared, cooked and, above all, consumed convivially, as of old. Give thanks and enjoy!

RECIPES FOR A BUFFET

Chickpea and Lentil Salad
Date Bread Twists
Nets of Galilee
Stuffed Vine Leaves
Hummus
Almond and Pear Creams

CHICKPEA AND LENTIL SALAD

This is an ideal vegetarian mainstay for a Biblical buffet table. Fruit and nuts were popular additions and merchants would have many varieties to trade. Dried chickpeas require to be soaked overnight and boiled for 2.5−3 hours until soft. Alternatively you can use tinned pulses that are cooked ready-to-eat and very handy.

INGREDIENTS

1 medium can cooked chickpeas, drained
50 g brown lentils, cooked & drained
1 tblsp mint leaves, chopped
Pinch of salt
Freshly milled pepper
25 g pine nuts
25 g almonds
25 g raisins
30 mls (2 tblsps) olive oil
The juice of 1 lemon
1 tblsp coriander leaves, chopped

METHOD

- Combine ingredients in a large bowl and allow to stand at room temperature for 30 minutes for flavours to develop.
- Taste to check seasoning and serve.

Serves 6 as a side salad or double ingredients for 12.

"Day by day, as they spent much time together in the temple, they broke bread at home and ate their food with glad and generous hearts ..." [Acts 2:46]

6

DATE BREAD TWISTS

Bread was a very valuable source of energy. Unleavened bread, the forerunner of our pitta, was widely consumed. The Egyptians probably cooked with yeast – although not the "fast-acting yeasts" of today. In Jesus' time bread would have been cooked directly on hot stones from the embers. Symbolic bread references occur throughout the Bible – even Bethlehem means The House of Bread.

INGREDIENTS
225 g spelt flour
Half a level teaspoon salt
1 x 6 g sachet easy-blend yeast
150 mls warm water
30 mls (2 tblsps) olive oil
6 large semi-dried dates, chopped

METHOD
- Preheat oven to 230°C/Gas No 8.
- Mix dry ingredients together in a large bowl.
- Add warm water and oil and mix together with a wooden spoon to make a soft dough.
- The dough should come away cleanly from the sides of the bowl – if too wet, add a little spelt flour; if too powdery, add a little more warm water.
- Knead the dough on a floured surface for a full 10 minutes to strengthen the gluten and create a smooth springy dough.
- Set aside in a warm place for 30 minutes to relax and rise.
- Knock back by kneading then divide the dough into 6.
- Roll out each section of dough into a "stick," twist and lay on a greased tray.
- Bake for approximately 8 minutes. They should be set and golden, and have a hollow sound when tapped on the underside.

Makes 6 or double ingredients for 12.

"Then he took a loaf of bread, and when he had given thanks, he broke it and gave it to them, saying, 'This is my body, which is given for you. Do this in remembrance of me.' And he did the same with the cup after supper, saying, 'This cup that is poured out for you is the new covenant in my blood' . . ." [Luke 22:19–20]

NETS OF GALILEE

Fishing was fundamental to life in Bible times, providing a plentiful harvest for the community and fishermen came to be associated with many parables: Loaves and Fishes, and the Storm with Jesus come to mind. The water's edge would be both market and meeting place and the many fires along the shore would cook the catch and provide food for locals and travellers alike.

"Then he ordered the crowds to sit down on the grass. Taking the five loaves and the two fish, he looked up to heaven, and blessed and broke the loaves, and gave them to the disciples, and the disciples gave them to the crowds. And all ate and were filled ..." [Matthew 14:19–20]

INGREDIENTS
6 sardines, scored diagonally with a sharp knife
Freshly milled pepper
A few sprigs of oregano
Pinch of salt
2 cloves of garlic, peeled & bruised
Olive oil for brushing

METHOD
- Preheat grill/barbecue.
- Brush fish with oil and rub with garlic. Season and grill for approx 3 minutes per side, depending on the size of the fish. The fish is cooked when the flesh is opaque and flakes easily with a fork.

Allow one fish per person and serve with wholemeal pitta breads.

STUFFED VINE LEAVES

Wrapping foods in vine leaves was not only highly attractive but also very functional. They are best steamed to retain the moisture in the leaves. Spinach leaves or spring greens can be successfully substituted.

INGREDIENTS

30 mls (2 tblsps) olive oil
1 onion, peeled & chopped
1 stick of celery
A generous pinch of freshly-grated nutmeg
1 cooked beetroot, peeled & diced
25 g sultanas
Pinch of mixed herbs
Freshly-milled pepper & a pinch of salt
25 g (2 tblsps) brown breadcrumbs
125 mls grape juice
1 pack of vine leaves (available vacuum packed from a
   delicatessen) or fresh leaves steamed to lightly pre-cook.

METHOD

- Heat oil in a frying pan or wok and sauté onion and celery until soft.
- Add beetroot, sultanas and seasoning and combine well.
- Stir in breadcrumbs and juice to form a pliable mix perfect for filling leaves.
- Spread out each leaf (or 2 depending on size) and place a heaped spoonful of mix in centre.
- Roll up firmly and serve warm or cold on the buffet. Alternatively place in steamer side by side and reheat for 6 minutes until piping hot to serve.

Makes 6 portions or double ingredients for 12.

"Go therefore into the main streets, and invite everyone you find to the wedding banquet." [Matthew 22:9]

HUMMUS

Chickpeas, grown in Palestine in Bible times and still produced today, are very versatile for cooking. Tahini is a sesame seed paste associated with Middle Eastern cookery and a classic hummus ingredient.

INGREDIENTS

1 medium can cooked
  chickpeas
The juice of 1 lemon
1 clove of garlic, peeled &
  crushed
Freshly-milled black pepper
30–45 mls (2–3 tblsps)
  olive oil
30 mls (2 tblsps) tahini

METHOD

• Place all ingredients in a
  blender and liquidise to
  make a rough paste.

Serves 6 or double
ingredients for 12 with
celery sticks and slices of
date twists.

"So, whether you eat or drink, or whatever you do, do everything for the glory of God." [I Corinthians 10:31]

Almond and Pear Creams

Thanks to the high cost of cane sugar Hebrew teeth were spared much dental decay, sweetening being provided by honey. Indeed, according to Genesis, Canaan was "a land flowing with milk and honey". Then as now, bees foraging amidst the multitude of wild flowers would produce honeys of many flavours resulting in subtle variations in regional dishes.

Ingredients
3 pears, peeled,
   halved & cored
1 tblsp local honey
25 g ground almonds
25 g icing sugar
Zest and juice of
   1 orange
1 medium tub sour
   cream

Method
- Place honey in a pan along with about an inch of water.
- Place in pears (tightly), along with zest, and cover with lid. Steam gently until pears are tender but intact.
- Place pears, upturned, in a dish. Reduce syrup and drizzle over pears.
- Combine almonds, sugar and sufficient juice to make a marzipan consistency.
- Place a nugget in each pear hollow and serve chilled with sour cream.

Serves 6 or double ingredients for 12.

Recipes for Dining

Pottage of Lentils
St Peter's Grill
Passover Lamb
Honeyed Fruits of the Holy Land

POTTAGE OF LENTILS

The agrarians in Bible times were thrifty and inventive – discovering, through necessity, how to make frugal meals enjoyable. Lentils were very popular and a rich source of protein. They ripened in June and July and would be stored to give year-round sustenance. This pottage can be vegetarian by substituting vegetable bouillon for the chicken stock.

"When he was at the table with them, he took bread, blessed and broke it, and gave it to them. Then their eyes were opened, and they recognised him ..."
[Luke 24:30–31]

INGREDIENTS
30 mls (2 tblsps) olive oil
1 onion, peeled & chopped
2 stalks of celery, diced
2 carrots, sliced
1 tblsp chopped coriander
2 litres chicken stock
Freshly-milled pepper
Pinch of salt
1 teaspoon ground cumin
375 g red lentils

METHOD
- Heat oil in large pan and sauté onions.
- Add celery and carrot and sauté gently in the pan to soften.
- Add lentils, spices and stock and allow to simmer for 25 minutes until lentils are soft.
- Stir in herbs and serve scattered with cubes of bread if wished.

Serves 6.

St. peter's Grill

The shimmering seas were bountiful and the fish would be carried ashore in baskets of twisted rope. Any fish can be used but sea bream bears a close resemblance to the contemporary sea harvest. Spinach or spring greens can deputise for vine leaves!

Ingredients
6 sea bream, gutted
Pinch of salt
Freshly-milled pepper
A small bunch of thyme
A small bunch of oregano
A small bunch of rosemary
Olive oil for brushing
Spinach leaves

Method
- Season fish and place herbs in cavities.
- Brush with oil and wrap in spinach leaves. Brush again.
- Preheat grill pan and cook sea bream for approx 8 minutes each side under a medium heat. The fish is cooked when the flesh is opaque and flakes easily with a fork.

Serves 6.

"When they had gone ashore, they saw a charcoal fire there, with fish on it, and bread. Jesus said to them, 'Bring some of the fish that you have just caught ... Come and have breakfast'." [John 21:9–10, 12a]

PASSOVER LAMB

The Paschal Lamb was the lamb sacrificed at the first Passover and was symbolic of Christ. It would be roasted over the open fire and nothing was to be left. Sheep played a key role in life, providing flesh, skins and wool, and featured in many parables – Christ or God representing the shepherd and the people, his flock.

"Jesus said to them, 'The wedding-guests cannot fast while the bridegroom is with them, can they?'"
[Mark 2:19]

INGREDIENTS

Whole leg of lamb
3 cloves of garlic, peeled & chopped
Sprigs of rosemary
Freshly-milled pepper & a light seasoning of salt
2 bunches of spring onions, cleaned and outer leaves removed
4 cooked beetroots, quartered
4 medium carrots, cut into chunks

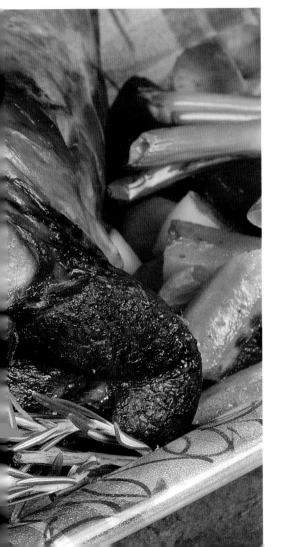

METHOD

- Preheat oven to 180°C/Gas No 5.
- Place lamb uncovered in oven and roast for a total of 25 minutes per pound plus 25 minutes to finish, then allow to rest for 15 minutes prior to serving.
- Check lamb from time to time. After the first hour, when it has started to cook, rub in garlic with the back of a spoon and season with pepper.
- For the last 40 minutes of cooking time, add vegetables to juices and cook until tender.

Serve with bread to mop up delicious juices.
Serves 6.

Honeyed Fruits of the Holy Land

Pomegranates were said to be "full of seeds and full of good deeds".
Their vibrant ruby seeds were commonly used in dishes and are now
known to have many health benefits. Wine production was common
and with spices from India many delicate desserts were created.

Ingredients
Seeds of 2 pomegranates
6 figs, quartered
150 g dates, fresh or semi-dried without stones
3 glasses red wine
1 stick of cinnamon
1 dessertspoon local runny honey

Method
- Place fruits in a pan and gently poach in sufficient red wine to cover the prepared fruit, along with a stick of cinnamon and honey until fruits mellow but still retain their shape.

Serve warm or chilled. Serves 6.